W9-DFT-981

James Oglethorpe

Humanitarian and Soldier

Colonial Leaders

Lord Baltimore
English Politician and Colonist

Benjamin Banneker
American Mathematician and Astronomer

Sir William Berkeley
Governor of Virginia

William Bradford
Governor of Plymouth Colony

Jonathan Edwards
Colonial Religious Leader

Benjamin Franklin
American Statesman, Scientist, and Writer

Anne Hutchinson
Religious Leader

Cotton Mather
Author, Clergyman, and Scholar

Increase Mather
Clergyman and Scholar

James Oglethorpe
Humanitarian and Soldier

William Penn
Founder of Democracy

Sir Walter Raleigh
English Explorer and Author

Caesar Rodney
American Patriot

John Smith
English Explorer and Colonist

Miles Standish
Plymouth Colony Leader

Peter Stuyvesant
Dutch Military Leader

George Whitefield
Clergyman and Scholar

Roger Williams
Founder of Rhode Island

John Winthrop
Politician and Statesman

John Peter Zenger
Free Press Advocate

Revolutionary War Leaders

John Adams
Second U.S. President

Ethan Allen
Revolutionary Hero

Benedict Arnold
Traitor to the Cause

King George III
English Monarch

Nathanael Greene
Military Leader

Nathan Hale
Revolutionary Hero

Alexander Hamilton
First U.S. Secretary of the Treasury

John Hancock
President of the Continental Congress

Patrick Henry
American Statesman and Speaker

John Jay
First Chief Justice of the Supreme Court

Thomas Jefferson
Author of the Declaration of Independence

John Paul Jones
Father of the U.S. Navy

Lafayette
French Freedom Fighter

James Madison
Father of the Constitution

Francis Marion
The Swamp Fox

James Monroe
American Statesman

Thomas Paine
Political Writer

Paul Revere
American Patriot

Betsy Ross
American Patriot

George Washington
First U.S. President

Famous Figures of the Civil War Era

Jefferson Davis
Confederate President

Frederick Douglass
Abolitionist and Author

Ulysses S. Grant
Military Leader and President

Stonewall Jackson
Confederate General

Robert E. Lee
Confederate General

Abraham Lincoln
Civil War President

William Sherman
Union General

Harriet Beecher Stowe
Author of Uncle Tom's Cabin

Sojourner Truth
Abolitionist, Suffragist, and Preacher

Harriet Tubman
Leader of the Underground Railroad

James Oglethorpe

Humanitarian and Soldier

Cookie Lommel

Arthur M. Schlesinger, jr.
Senior Consulting Editor

Chelsea House Publishers

Philadelphia

Produced by Pre-Press Company, Inc., East Bridgewater, MA 02333

CHELSEA HOUSE PUBLISHERS
Editor in Chief Stephen Reginald
Production Manager Pamela Loos
Art Director Sara Davis
Director of Photography Judy L. Hasday
Managing Editor James D. Gallagher
Senior Production Editor J. Christopher Higgins

Staff for *JAMES OGLETHORPE*
Project Editor Anne Hill
Associate Art Director Takeshi Takahashi
Series Design Keith Trego

The Chelsea House World Wide Web address is http://www.chelseahouse.com

First Printing
1 3 5 7 9 8 6 4 2

Library of Congress Cataloging-in-Publication Data
Lommel, Cookie.
   James Oglethorpe/Cookie Lommel.
      p.cm. — (Colonial Leaders)
      Includes bibliographical references and index.
   Summary: A biography of English founder and first governor of the colony of Georgia who was active in politics and penal reform.
      ISBN 0-7910-5963-4 (HC); 0-7910-6120-5 (PB)
      1. Oglethorpe, James Edward, 1696—1785—Juvenile literature.
      2. Georgia —History—Colonial period, ca. 1600-1775—Juvenile literature.
      3. Governors—Georgia—Biography—Juvenile literature. [1. Oglethorpe, James Edward, 1696-1785. 2. Governors. 3. Georgia—History—Colonial period, ca. 1600-1775.] I. Title. II. Series

F289.O37 L66 2000
975.8'02'092—dc21
[BB]
                                                          00-038382

Publisher's Note: In Colonial and Revolutionary War America, there were no standard rules for spelling, punctuation, capitalization, or grammar. Some of the quotations that appear in the Colonial Leaders and Revolutionary War Leaders series come from original documents and letters written during this time in history. Original quotations reflect writing inconsistencies of the period.

Contents

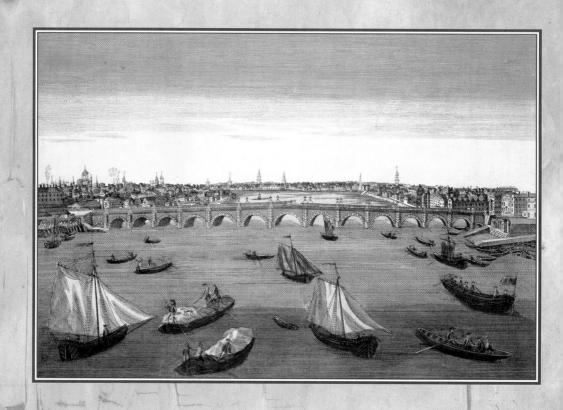

At the time of James Oglethorpe's birth, England was enjoying great prosperity as a result of her large shipping industry and vast military power on the seas. As part of England's wealthy society, the Oglethorpe family had a great sense of loyalty to the crown and the government.

A Privileged Beginning

December 22, 1696, was a cold and snowy day but the archbishop of Canterbury did not mind the weather. As a religious leader, it was his job to baptize newborn babies, and the archbishop joyfully prepared to **christen** a baby boy. Young James Edward Oglethorpe was born while his family was visiting their winter home in London, England. James was the Oglethorpes' tenth child and their fifth son. The entire family was very excited about the new baby.

The Oglethorpes were a very wealthy family and trusted members of England's upper class. James's mother was one of Queen Anne's ladies-in-waiting, a group of noblewomen who served the queen. James's father and brothers were members of Parliament, England's government.

The Oglethorpes' loyalty to their country was strong. Family members felt it was their duty to serve in the military. The children were expected to share this sense of duty. Children in the 18th century had short childhoods. More was expected in those times. Poor children were sent out to work, sometimes as young as age six or seven. Parents chose the jobs their children would do.

Rich children, like James, also did many of the same things grown-ups did. James's father was a general in the king's army. He was killed in combat in 1702, when James was only 6 years old. Young James followed the family **tradition** of becoming a soldier. When he was 10 years old, James became a foot guard for the queen. At 15, he entered Lompres Military Academy near Paris, France.

It was not uncommon to see small children working long days in businesses such as this printing shop. Most often, a parent would decide where a child was going to work and what trade they would learn.

James's mother had to raise all of her children alone. These were very difficult times for the Oglethorpe family.

James spent much of his childhood dreaming of a military career. However, his mother had different ideas. In 1714 she sent him to study at Oxford University. He had a talent for learning languages easily, which would help him greatly in his future. James also loved to have fun. Archery was his hobby. He was often seen around London practicing his sport.

A war between Turkey and Austria broke out in 1716, and many young men volunteered to join the Austrian army. James's dream of a military career became real. Being a soldier was part of his family heritage. He would soon be one of those brave young men who would join this fight. He was accepted onto the staff of the field marshal. When the field marshal was wounded, James helped carry him from the battlefield. James was promoted to lieutenant colonel for his brave deeds. This was quite an achievement, as he was only 21 years old at the time.

James's oldest brother, Lewis, was killed at the Battle of Schellenberg, and another brother,

Theophilus, died in England. When James returned from the war, he inherited the family estate which was called Westbrook. In his new role as a leader in the community, he began to take interest in local affairs and funded many projects, such as donating money to repair the communal fire engines and buy new buckets. James also had a green thumb and a love for gardening. The attention he **devoted** to Westbrook resulted in it becoming the largest vineyard in England.

Like his father and his brothers before him, James became a member of Parliament. He was only 26 years old. His election in 1722 was a very heated one, and James battled his political enemies with his sword as well as with words. Dueling was very common during the 18th century, and men thought that it was important to defend their honor. The well respected Oglethorpe family followed such customs. A hot-headed group, his father and brothers would never back away from a fight for honor. One day, James passed two of his political **rivals** on the street. An argument started and the men drew swords. James wounded one man in the stomach and the other in the thigh. He was arrested but later that year he was able to take his seat in Parliament.

James gained great respect in Parliament and was appointed to 42 parliamentary committees. His political activities were aimed at a consideration of the poor, and he gave much to better the lives of ordinary citizens in England. In his first year in Parliament, James sponsored a law to rent cottages to the poor. This legislation stopped many landowners from destroying inexpensive homes on their estates.

James also became involved in the improvement of prisons, which during that time were unclean, overcrowded, and breeding grounds for diseases. James had a personal reason to care about prisons. His friend, Robert Castell, a writer who had published a very good book but had made no money, was put into a debtors' prison because he could not pay his bills. In England

Prisons in the 1700s were dirty, overcrowded, and a breeding ground for disease. Criminals as well as those who could not pay off their debts were put in jail.

during that time, there were more people than there were jobs. People who had no jobs and could not pay their bills went to jail.

When Robert Castell went to jail, the warden put him in an area with people who had many diseases. There, he caught smallpox and died. James blamed the warden for his friend's death, and he formed a special committee to investigate the prison system. The committee found that prisoners were chained, tortured, and left in rooms with little air. After James brought these horrible conditions to light, several debtors were released from jail. However, Parliament did not stop putting people in debtors' prison until 1869.

James soon found that solving the problem of people who owed money was not easy and that letting people in debt out of jail created other problems. People without jobs or food were now living on the streets of London. James thus turned his attention to the issues of unemployment and poverty.

His answer was to start a colony in the New World. Using skills that he had learned as a politician, landowner, gardener, and soldier, James formed the Georgia Society (named for King George II) in 1730. His goal was to give poor citizens of England a new start in a new land. Starting a colony for the poor was not an original idea. John Smith had begun the Virginia colony in 1606 for the same reasons.

The new colony was good for both England and its common people. Georgia was also an excellent location for England's military, and the colony would help protect England's interests in the New World. The Spanish, who were enemies of England, had troops in Florida, very close to Georgia. The location and climate of Georgia were excellent for growing crops and the newcomers would be able to support themselves growing rice, silk, and tobacco.

There were other benefits to creating a colony in Georgia. Many people from Europe had come to England seeking religious freedom. James and his committee thought that they should also be invited to join the new colony.

In spite of all these reasons, it was still difficult for James to convince Parliament to start the colony. England was not eager to pay the passage

In 1732 George II awarded a land grant to James's committee to form a colony in the New World. In honor of the king, James named the colony Georgia. The colony was to become a place for those who were in debt but wanted to begin a new life.

for such a group and support them until their crops grew.

Eventually, on June 9, 1732, George II awarded the land to James's committee, which thus became the trustees of the Georgia colony. The trustees, including James, agreed that they would not accept a salary and they turned down land and personal gain to form the colony. The trustees designed a seal for the colony, which read, in Latin, "Not for Themselves but for Others." Georgia was to be unique—a land of common people. This colony was unlike most of the other colonies, which had been started to benefit the landowners.

James and the other trustees began to raise money to start the colony. Not all of the **contributions** were in the form of money. Hoes, plows, spades, and other tools were donated and the colonists also received plants, seeds, clothing, and equipment to create a new life in Georgia.

After nearly two months at sea, James Oglethorpe's ship, the *Anne*, arrived in the port of Charles Town, South Carolina, in November of 1732. The city, which today is called Charleston, remains an important Atlantic seaport.

Forming a Colony

On November 17, 1732, 114 passengers left England on a 200-ton ship called the *Anne* to start the Georgia colony. The ship was crowded but the passengers and crew stayed healthy, except for two sick children who died during the trip. The group arrived in Charles Town, South Carolina, on January 13, 1733.

The South Carolina General Assembly helped the newcomers **establish** the Georgia colony. The assembly voted to give the group hogs, cattle, rice, small boats, and money. While the travelers rested from their long sea journey, James Oglethorpe went

The colonists expected to make silk in Georgia. They brought special mulberry trees to the colony because silkworms can only live in these trees. Silk is made from the cocoons of the silkworm. The art of growing silk comes from China. For years, only the Chinese knew the secret of how to make silk. It is believed that Chinese monks brought the silkworm to other countries.

to explore Georgia—the last, and the largest, of the 13 colonies founded by England. Today, Georgia is the largest state east of the Mississippi River.

The first major area to be established became the city of Savannah. James started a community garden, which he called the Trustees Garden. It was modeled after the Chelsea Botanical Garden in London. Farmers were sent from England to grow mulberry trees to provide a habitat for silkworms, grapes for wine, and other crops. Most of these crops could not adjust to the Georgia climate. However, from this experiment came peaches and cotton—the two crops that would become a major source of income for the people of Georgia. Raising cattle and trading fur

The practice of trading fur and other goods
with the Native Americans served not only as
a reliable source of income for the colonists
but also helped form a strong alliance which
Oglethorpe would later use in his battles with
the Spanish.

The peach has a long history. First grown in China, it spread through Asia to Spain and Mexico. It was a symbol of long life. Peach seeds or pits were brought to America by the Spanish. Today there are 300 different kinds of peaches. They grow best in warm climates, like Georgia's. Georgia is known as the Peach State.

with the Native Americans also helped the colony grow.

James began to plan the building of the city of Savannah—a system of squares that were really miniature parks. Houses, churches, and businesses surrounded each square. Today Savannah still has 23 squares that make up its historic district.

A few houses were built by the summer of 1733, but life was very hard the first year. There was a shortage of clean water and disease spread in the hot climate. Many settlers died.

Luckily, a half-English, half-Native American woman named Mary Musgrove introduced James to Chief Tomochichi of the nearby Yamacraw tribe. They became life-long friends, and the chief helped the colonists **survive.** James invited the chief and some of his family to

England where they were treated very well, at great expense. A meeting was even arranged with King George. Chief Tomochichi was very happy with the English, and he wanted his people to be educated in some of their ways. James wanted the Native Americans to grant him rights to certain land areas in Georgia. An agreement that both groups could live under was reached and **treaties** of peace and friendship were signed before the Native Americans left England.

But the Georgia colony still had problems. The trustees did not have a realistic understanding of life in

Most women in the Georgia colony assumed the duties of caring for their families and homes: cooking, cleaning, and raising children. Mary Musgrove, was different— she aided in the colony's formation.

Mary was responsible for the friendship that formed between James Oglethorpe and Chief Tomochichi. Mary was a good advisor, and Oglethorpe depended on her to tell him about problems in the colony and how to fix them.

Though women in the colony were not allowed to own property, Mary was given a grant of 500 acres because her contributions to the growth of Georgia had been so important.

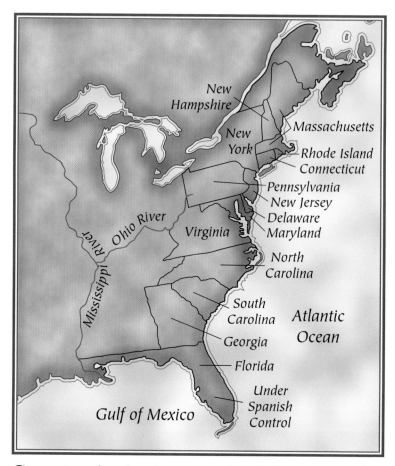

Georgia, the furthest south of the original 13 colonies, has a climate very different from that of northern Europe. This was another difficulty for the settlers to overcome.

Georgia and the difficulties of growing food. While there were good harvests some years, food had to be brought to Georgia from England during the bad times. Many of the settlers were city people who were not used to farm life and could not handle the hard work on the frontier. Consequently, Georgia did not grow as quickly as the trustees had hoped.

In addition, the colonists had to deal with the issue of slavery. James had forbidden the colonists to own slaves, and the practice was already being attacked in England. During that same period, German settlers in Philadelphia were also taking a strong stand against slavery. The Georgia colonists, however, did not agree. They

More than half of the people who came to America in the 18th century came as **indentured** servants. They provided much-needed labor for the colonies. Arriving from England, Germany, Ireland, and other European countries, they worked to pay back the money spent to get to the New World. They signed agreements with their masters to work for a number of years, usually from five to seven. They worked on farms and as servants in homes. Some were able to serve their time and become landowners themselves, but many continued to be poor and unskilled. Although they were not slaves, many were treated just as badly.

felt that Georgia could not develop into a strong colony without the help of slaves.

Many people came to the colonies seeking riches, either by trading with the Native Americans or owning land. When they owned land, they needed people to work on it. Unfortunately, this created a climate for slavery. The Georgia colonists saw other colonies growing rich with the use of slave labor and they also wanted the same easy life.

Because these colonists only had their eyes on riches, they lost sight of the fact that they would become people *owning* other people. They also forgot that they themselves had been targets of **persecution** in their homelands.

There were other disagreements. The drinking of hard liquor had been banned by James Oglethorpe and only wine and beer were still allowed in the Georgia colony. Although some people had died from drinking brandy, rum, and gin, the colonists were still unhappy there was no alcohol. James and the trustees were trying to protect the settlers by banning slaves as well as liquor, but the colonists disliked these rules.

Many other problems took place in the Georgia colony. There was constant illness, probably due to disease-carrying mosquitoes, which reduced the colonists' energy and ability to work. In July 1733, the sickness was at its worst.

A ship carrying 42 Jewish passengers came to Savannah. Though they had not been sent by the trustees, they asked to join the colony. The custom was to welcome all new settlers, except for Catholics, the only religious group that was not allowed. The reason was that many of the colonists had been thrown out of their homelands by the Catholics.

The colonists were particularly lucky with these newcomers. Within the group was a doctor, a person whose help they desperately needed. Dr. Samuel Nunis was immediately able to treat those with fevers and other illnesses, and many colonists quickly recovered their health. The Jewish settlers made other con-

Children in the colonies had many chores, such as taking care of the farm animals and helping with the gardening and the harvest. Their mothers were also happy to have them help with the drying of fruits and vegetables. Boys helped their fathers carve furniture.

Schooling was very different during that time. Since most people did not live near a school, parents had to teach children to read and write or hire a traveling teacher to help. Children still had time to play simple games and they enjoyed storytelling and singing.

tributions to the colony and many of them went on to become some of Savannah's leading citizens.

The problems of the colony weren't over, however. English laws prevented the colony from trading products which would directly compete with products that England traded. There were still more problems. In the winter of 1734, a ship arrived with Irish convicts to supply needed manpower. Within two weeks, one male and one female convict were each charged with murder.

Some help came from an unlikely place as more settlers arrived in Georgia in 1734. Among them was a group of German-speaking Luther-

Children were expected to help with the chores of the household. The young girls would assist their mothers in tasks such as drying fruit or mending clothes, while the boys would help with outdoor chores.

ans from the mountains near Salzburg, Austria. They had been driven from their homeland when the Roman Catholic archbishop of Salzburg forced them to leave. Thousands of people were made homeless and many fled to Germany, Sweden, Holland, and England. The trustees of the Georgia colony offered to send several families to Georgia. The first group traveled by foot from their home in Salzburg to the port of Rotterdam in Holland. It was a very hard journey and they lost all of their belongings.

When the Austrians reached Georgia, they were very thankful. The colonists heartily welcomed them. James Oglethorpe directed the new arrivals to the area that would become the town of Ebenezer, where they would make their new home. James provided each family with a large amount of beef, fresh vegetables, and fruit. James's personal attention was never forgotten by the Austrians.

The new settlers were, in turn, good for the Georgia colony. They were not strangers to farming and many of them had raised cows and sheep in their homeland. They were hard-working people who turned Ebenezer into one of the most successful towns in Georgia. They founded the first orphanage in the colony and also started the first Sunday school.

Other newcomers who helped the Georgia colony grow stronger were Scottish Highlanders who settled in the town of Darien in 1735. This group of 150 survivors of a military conflict in Scotland were later important in the defense of Georgia. They were highly praised by the trustees for building two forts in the colony. The Highlanders in Darien were handsomely rewarded for their fine service with 100 pounds sterling of English money. The Highlanders, who were Presbyterians, brought their own minister to the New World. Once again, the new colony in Georgia provided a home

The colonists brought seeds to plant crops in Georgia—among them Georgia's famous peaches.

The settlers also ate beans, corn, potatoes, grapes, apples, and blueberries. They were afraid to drink the water, which often made them sick. They thought it better to drink fruit juices, cider, and beer. In England, people who ate vegetables were considered poor, a belief that was also brought to Georgia. So beef, vension, fish, lamb, and turkey were part of their diets. The Native Americans showed them pumpkins and squash. The colonists had not seen these vegetables before, but they quickly realized that these were a tasty addition to their meals.

to a growing mix of people, each with something unique to offer.

James Oglethorpe's idea of how a colony could be successful was beginning to change. Life was different from what he had expected before he had spent a few years in the New World. Though he was able to start several towns in Georgia, the colony was still far from being a lasting community. South Carolina was Georgia's only friendly border. On the other borders, both the Spanish and the French were waiting for Georgia to fall. James knew it was possible that Georgia might not survive. But he learned from his mistakes and worked hard to make the colony a success.

However, there were many problems facing a small colony that wanted to become self-sufficient. The trustees, who were far away in England, didn't anticipate the expenses that would be needed to keep a colony running. As many daily problems in the colony took more and more of his time, James did not communicate regularly with the trustees. He would send bills without explaining how the money was being spent. The trustees thus became worried because they did not know what was happening in Georgia. They began to lose interest in the colony, causing it to have financial problems.

In 1734 James returned to England to raise money for the Georgia colony. Using his skills of **persuasion,** James got the trustees and Parliament to issue a grant of £25,000 for the colony.

James knew he had valuable allies among the neighboring tribes of the colony. He would often exchange gifts as tokens of friendship with Native American leaders. By creating strong ties with Chief To-mochichi, he gained favor with the other surrounding tribes.

3
Native American Friends

Of all his many efforts in the colony, James Oglethorpe had the most success in making friends with the Native Americans. Before he went to Georgia, relations between the Native Americans and the settlers had not been easy. When the English first came to the area, they were ruthless and dishonest with the Native Americans. This angered the Native Americans and they no longer wanted to trade their deer and other animal skins, which were popular with the Europeans.

It was not the first time this had happened. The French and the Spanish had also treated the Native

Americans badly. The problems developed into a full-scale Indian war between 1715 and 1716. This war almost wiped out the colony of South Carolina.

But James had a different relationship with the Native Americans and he wanted Georgians to develop trade with them. James was always very fair in all trading and gave many gifts to the Native Americans. He also used his ties to Chief Tomochichi to gain favor with other surrounding tribes. James realized that the settlers in the colony were outnumbered by the Native Americans. Since the French and the Spanish were his enemies, it was very important that the Native Americans remained his **allies.**

By then, the French and the Spanish were also trying to make friends with the Native Americans. They wanted to take over the Georgia territory. Keeping danger at bay was not an easy task, but James managed it well. When James returned to Georgia after a visit to England, he found that in spite of efforts by the

French and the Spanish, Chief Tomochichi had remained a faithful friend. The chief helped James form a good relationship with the Creeks, who also promised him their loyalty.

Eager to have the support of all the Native American tribes in the area if war should break out, James also met with the Chickasaw chief and presented him with the coat off of his back. This was an important symbol that delighted the chief. James also gave many gifts to the tribe's women and children.

In addition to befriending the Native Americans, James also formed other ways to protect Georgia. He explored the dangerous areas down the coast. He needed to establish a town on Georgia's southern border in order to defend the colony. He also wanted to look for two missing Englishmen who were reported to be meeting with the Spanish for treaty talks.

Setting sail on the *Symond,* James landed on Cockspur Island, near Savannah. He was **anxious** to sail further to St. Simon's Island. However, the ship's owner refused to go through places he had never been. **Desperate** to get moving, James bought another ship. He hired the most experienced men he could find and sailed ahead along the coast.

James planned to build 20 forts to defend the Georgia colony along the coast. In order to help, Chief Tomochichi joined James in exploring the islands of the south. They went to Jekyll Island, which the English had already explored. Later, they came to an island that Chief Tomochichi suggested they name Cumberland Island in honor of a special friend whom the chief met during his visit to England. James built a fort called St. Andrew on Cumberland Island.

As they moved to the south, James and Chief Tomochichi went to an island the Spanish called Santa Maria, which James renamed Amelia. They continued onto the island of San Juan, which James renamed St. George. There, he found the crumbling walls of an old fort. He ordered his men to rebuild it.

Coastal Georgia was filled with plants and animals that the colonists had never seen before. As Oglethorpe and his settlers were traveling to St. Simon's Island, they saw a beautiful display of large trees draped with Spanish moss.

In the area of St. George, Native American scouts reported to James that there were campfires nearby. Thinking that the campfires belonged to the Spanish military, the scouts wanted to make a surprise attack. James would not agree without more facts. He was wise to be cautious. The next morning, they discovered that the campfires belonged to one of the missing Englishmen and his crew, whose boat had sunk. The other missing man was being held by the Spanish.

Oglethorpe then set sail with more settlers for St. Simon's Island, a beautiful place with large oak trees draped with Spanish moss. The new settlers were excited by its different wildlife–including turkeys and alligators, which they had not seen before. They stayed to build up the settlement of Frederica, where James built Fort St. Simon's, his third powerful fort. James claimed more and more land that the Spanish felt belonged to them. A war with Spain seemed likely.

There were many small conflicts. When James sent a messenger to the Spanish governor, he heard a rumor that the Spanish had taken his messenger prisoner. He went to St.

George to find out. While waiting on the island, he sensed that the Spanish were ready to attack. James and his men saved themselves with a clever trick. They had brought two kinds of cannons with them; one kind was a little quieter than the other. Ships always fired a seven-gun salute to forts, who answered with a five-gun blast. So James fired his quieter cannon seven times and made his louder cannons answer with five shots. This way, the Spanish thought that he had a big ship coming to their rescue and they left him alone.

As part of his defense of the young Georgia colony, James wanted to forge more friendships with the Native Americans who lived in the area. He thought these alliances would be important in the worsening **situation** with Spain.

He was right. James wrote to the trustees that he had received information that the Spanish were trying to bribe the Creek nation. Also, unfair trading practices were creating trouble. To help solve the problem, James's Native

James Oglethorpe

Oglethorpe gained great respect from Native American tribes for his fairness and leadership abilities. The tribes promised to be loyal to the British crown and to him, in exchange for his promise to respect their right to keep their own territory.

American friends arranged a meeting for him with a large group of Native American nations.

Over 7,000 warriors—from the Creek, Chickasaw, Choctaw, Cherokee, Yamacraw, and other great tribes—met with James during a 10-day ceremony. James's Native American friends signed an important treaty with him. They again promised their loyalty to him and to the British Crown. The tribes confirmed the grants of land they had made several years before. In return, James promised to stay out of the territory saved by the Native Americans for their personal use.

This treaty was a great personal victory for James. It was made possible by his reputation for fairness and by the high respect in which his leadership was held. He had shown courage by taking the hard trip into uncertain territory to protect Georgia.

The city of Savannah was built on a system of squares that are actually miniature parks. Today, 23 of the original squares still exist in Savannah's historic district.

4

A Clever Leader

James Oglethorpe did not know that a war was brewing between Spain and England until he received an urgent message: England was being forced into a war with Spain. These two countries had been bitter rivals for the wealth of the New World for many years. Now Spain's position as a world power was weakening, while England's power was increasing. This fight would have a strong impact on the Georgia colony.

Spain had an agreement limiting the number of English ships that could trade with America. Many English shipowners ignored these laws and simply

smuggled goods they wanted to sell into America. It was difficult to catch these smugglers. If the Spanish did manage to capture one, they punished him harshly. When they caught an English ship captain named Robert Jenkins, they cut off his ear as an example to other smugglers. Jenkins complained to England's Parliament. There was nationwide anger about Spain's actions. In October 1739, England went to war against Spain. The fight would be called the War of Jenkins' Ear.

Since James knew he did not have enough soldiers to fight the Spanish, he called upon his loyal Native American friends. Unfortunately, he had to go to war without his much-valued friend and ally, Chief Tomochichi, who died on October 5, 1739. Some stories say that Tomochichi was 89 when he died; others claim he was 97. Because he had been such a good friend to the settlers, Chief Tomochichi was buried in Savannah, with James himself leading the funeral march.

Chief Tomochichi left his adopted son, Toon-ahowi, as leader of the Yamacraw tribe and it was to him that James turned to for help in fighting the Spanish. Toonahowi was as good a friend to the Georgia colony as his father. The new chief gave James as many men as he could spare, and then he sent messengers to the Creek tribes, asking them to help too.

James then gathered men from the colony, particularly the fierce Scottish Highlanders he had helped to settle in Darien. They had military experience, which would be needed to fight the Spanish. James was determined to capture the Spanish fort in St. Augustine.

But James still did not have the men he needed to face the Spanish, who had a large, well-trained body of men in the New World. James needed more help. He turned to his neighbor, South Carolina, hoping that the governor could give him 1,000 men as well as food, guns, and other supplies. Most of all, James needed army engineers. These soldiers were trained to build all the things needed for war. They would build bridges, walls, and trenches to surround a fort in order to protect it.

While James waited for an answer from South Carolina, he wrote to England asking for help, too. He needed big guns, like cannons, from the king, as well as boats and horses for the long trip to St. Augustine. He did not have all of the tools for war in the Georgia colony.

Before England or South Carolina answered James, the Spanish attacked his fort on Amelia Island. Two men were killed. James raised a small force of Highlanders, Native Americans, and the few regular soldiers in Georgia. With these men, he set out for St. Augustine to fight back against the Spanish.

He wanted to capture the fort at St. Augustine, but he only had 200 men. The soldiers in his small army also got sick from fever. But James did what he could, chasing some Spanish soldiers back to their fort at San Diego and then putting his men back inside Fort George. When

St. Augustine was a large and powerful fort built by the Spanish in what is now Florida. With few men and supplies, Oglethorpe was determined to capture St. Augustine and protect his colony from the invading Spanish.

the colony was at peace with Spain, James had agreed not to keep soldiers there. Now he returned his men to Fort George to guard against attack.

Badly needing more men, James returned to Frederica and then begged South Carolina for the men and supplies that he needed. He had received nothing from England. Yet, he was still determined to protect his colony. The South Carolinians were slow to help Georgia, afraid that if they sent men to fight the Spanish, the French would see it as an opportunity to attack South Carolina.

But James was a clever and brave military leader. While he waited for South Carolina to decide if it would help his colony, he raided the Spanish. He burned one of their forts to the ground and captured the other. These forts were named Fort Francis and Fort Picolata. Now James controlled an important land route to St. Augustine.

He used his success to talk South Carolina into sending him 600 men. He wanted to attack St. Augustine before the Spanish could send more men and supplies to protect it. But time was short. The men from South Carolina had not arrived when he attacked and captured Fort Diego. Then James received disastrous news. Spain had supplied the fort at St. Augustine with food, guns, and soldiers. James still had not gotten his aid from England.

James decided it was now or never. The Georgia colony might not survive if he did not take St. Augustine. Could the Spanish there beat both the Georgia and South Carolina troops? It was time to find out.

St. Augustine was a very old town. It had a history of **pirate** raids and Native American attacks. St. Augustine had also fought off the English. The Spanish had learned many ways to defend the town. In St. Augustine, they had built massive arches and lime pits to stop an attack. The city had large, overhead roofs to support the heaviest cannons. James did not think he had enough men for a direct attack, so he came up with another plan.

James noticed that the soldiers protecting nearby Anastasia Island were all on the end of

In the 18th century, pirates would often raid forts and settlements along the Atlantic coast such as St. Augustine in search of money and other valuable items.

the island nearest to St. Augustine. The other side of Anastasia had fewer soldiers, so James sent his troops there.

It was from this point that he planned to capture St. Augustine itself. James and his troops attacked a section of the island that they thought would drive the people into the center of St. Augustine. Instead, the gunshots drove them into the countryside. James continued the cannon fire, but the Spanish fired back. Neither side was very successful. A few prisoners were taken but many of them escaped. Many of James's Native American friends expected the town to be captured sooner. When

One type of pirate was a "privateer." They were encouraged by Britain to raid French and Spanish ships. As payment for their services, the crew would take a portion of the prize for themselves.

When European countries were at peace, the privateers were no longer wanted by the government and they became outlaws.

In the New World, pirates sailed along the eastern seaboard and raided merchant ships sailing from exotic locations like the Bahamas. As they headed toward the southern colonies, pirates took their cargoes of cocoa, sugar, and rum.

it wasn't, they left. The men from South Carolina were bothered by the heat and mosquitoes, and James was sick with a fever. Although he knew that the fight with the Spanish was not over, James retreated. He returned to his headquarters to watch and wait for more attacks.

The war with Spain was a frightening time that had a major impact on Georgia. Guards had to be on constant lookout for enemy ships. Women and children were moved to safer cities like Ebenezer and Salzburger. Many of the settlements were raided by Spanish ships, supplies and food were often very low, and trade was uncertain.

In 1742, a Spanish invasion fleet carrying about 3,000 men sailed from Havana, Cuba. Their orders were to destroy the Georgia and Carolina colonies. They planned to attack Frederica first.

But James was a resourceful leader. Even though his forces were outnumbered, they managed to fight off the enemy and save the Georgia colony. In order to beat the Spanish, James first took men and boats to the two forts on Cumberland Island. He had too few men to hold the forts, but he removed their supplies and ruined the fort's guns. When the Spanish took the fort, it was not as useful to them as they had hoped.

The next step was to ready the fort at Frederica for attack. James, along with his Highlanders, Toonahowi's warriors, and a small group of regular soldiers, soon met 200 Spanish soldiers on the road outside of the fort. James and his allies successfully fought off the attackers, but he knew more Spanish forces would be coming. Secretly posting a special guard, James and his men returned to the fort to silently watch, waiting for the right time to attack. They did not have to wait long.

The Spanish captain thought James and his troops had run away. He ordered his men to stack their guns and cook dinner for the night. Though there were about 300 Spanish soldiers,

James's special army attacked, killing most of the Spanish troops. The others ran into the marshlands, which is why this battle was later called Bloody Marsh.

James wanted to follow the battle with another surprise attack but discovered that a Frenchman and his forces had deserted and warned the Spanish leaders that there might be another attack. So James decided to save the colony with a clever trick. He sent a letter to the deserting Frenchman in which he made it look like the Frenchman was really James's spy, bringing lies to the Spaniards. He also claimed that the English were sending many big ships to rescue the colonies from Spain. Though they might not have believed the letter, Spanish lookouts saw a few English scout ships and mistook them for the military ships that James had claimed were coming. The Spanish troops retreated southward, and the colonies were saved. The Georgia colony, with the help of Toonahowi's warriors, had survived.

American history would have changed a great deal if Georgia had been lost to Spain. But the Spanish soldiers never mounted another big attack on Georgia, thanks to James Oglethorpe.

George III had taken the throne by the time that James returned to England. It is thought that Oglethorpe may have secretly supported the American colonists who later fought for independence from England.

Back to England

James Oglethorpe will always be remembered as a great soldier, a man who always did what he thought was needed even if it was hard to do. But in spite of being such a fierce fighter, he could also be a man of great kindness.

James formed the Georgia colony with clear goals. He wanted to establish communities where many different groups of people could make better lives for themselves. For this reason, he helped debtors, people who were punished because of their religions, and even convicts settle in Georgia. He maintained a respectful relationship with the nearby

Native Americans, who taught the colonists the way to survive in this hard New World with its strange climate, plants, and animals. Most importantly, he taught his settlers how to develop the ability to live without having to depend on others for aid.

Unlike many people of his time, James did not approve of slavery and the idea that one man could own another and live off of his work. He wanted people to work for themselves. When he readied Frederica to fight off the Spaniards, even the women who had stayed in the town were given a part of the wall that they were responsible for guarding. He saw the colonies as a place of great opportunity. The Old World did not have such promise left.

He may even have privately supported the American colonists who fought for independence from England many years after he had left Georgia. We know he did not judge them. He had spent many frustrating years himself trying to tell Parliament and the trustees what was really needed in the Georgia colony. He may have understood why the colonies broke away from the king. As an old man, he gave his best wishes to ambassador John Adams and the new government of the United States.

James had always given the Georgia colony his best efforts and did it without asking a lot for himself. He was the only founder of a colony who did not own any of its land. He made very little profit from Georgia. In fact, when he left his beloved colony for England in 1743, England owed him more than £70,000. He had spent his own money to build and protect the young colony. It is not known why James left Georgia, or if he ever planned to return to the colony. He may have left simply to sort out his own business affairs but he never again returned.

Today, there are many reminders of James Edward Oglethorpe in Georgia, however. There is Oglethorpe University in Atlanta, and Oglethorpe Avenue is still a main street in

Savannah. Many roads are named for James in Georgia and there is even the town of Fort Oglethorpe. His statue stands in Savannah and many pictures of him have been painted.

James Oglethorpe left an important mark on American history. But he was also an Englishman who was well-known in his own country. From 1743, when he left Georgia, until his death in 1785, he kept working very hard for what he believed in. He joined Granville Sharp to attack slavery in England. By now he believed that the German Quakers were right to think that slavery was wrong. The Germans understood this long before most of the world and they did not allow slavery in their Pennsylvania settlement.

Granville Sharp declared war on slavery in England after meeting a slave in 1765. In that year, a slave named Jonathan Strong had knocked on Sharp's door. Strong was a slave who had been badly beaten by his master and was near death. Sharp quickly got him to the

Oglethorpe agreed with the Quakers that slavery was wrong. He spent the last years of his life fighting for what he believed in.

hospital. After four long months, Strong was healthy again. Strong told Sharp how his master had kidnapped him and brought him to England. When Strong's master heard that he had recovered he paid two men to recapture him. Sharp was angry and he took the master to court. He said that since Strong was in England, he was no longer a slave. It took a long time, but Sharp succeeded in winning Strong's case. Sharp was then able to use this case to free others. He finally convinced the court that, "as soon as any slave sets foot on English territory, he is free."

James also fought against the cruelty of the **press-gang,** the English navy's way of getting new sailors. These fierce gangs walked the streets looking for men to serve on warships. They kidnapped men and forced them onto ships, leaving behind their wives and children. It was one of the most brutal things that could happen to a private citizen. James did not approve of the practice.

James served several more times as a member of Parliament. He wanted the government to make responsible choices. But these feelings may have stopped him from getting what he seems to have wanted most—more active military service.

By 1746, James had already faced two **court martials** in his military career. Both times he had been accused of military crimes by soldiers who had not liked their hard lives in Georgia. In both cases, James was found innocent. But in 1746, a more serious question of James's loyalty to England was raised.

During an English rebellion in which the grandson of James II, known as Bonnie Prince Charlie, claimed to be England's real king and not George II, James was accused of not chasing the rebel army quickly enough at a place called Shap. James said that his army was tired and did not have enough food. The court let him go free, but many people thought that he might have chased Bonnie Prince Charlie's army too slowly because he felt sorry for them. His own brother had been a supporter of the rebels.

The trial probably stopped James from getting what he wanted. Although James was raised to the rank of general, he was never given active service in the English army after the court martial. In 1755 he asked to form his old Georgia regiment again but the crown refused. When America fought England for their independence, he was not sent to the colonies. England was short of generals with experience in the New World but James was still kept at home.

James was restless. At the age of 48 he married Lady Elizabeth Wright and they settled in Cranham. But, by 1756, he was in active military service again, this time using a different name and fighting for a different army.

James was an English officer and not allowed to fight for other kings. Yet he took the name "Tibi," maybe after an island in the Savannah river, and fought the French for the German

When America fought for its independence, England was desperately short of generals with knowledge of the colonies. Though James was willing to assist England in its fight against the American colonies, his loyalty was questioned by the crown and he was not allowed back into active service.

Samuel Johnson was a famous traveler and author. His travels throughout the British Isles were documented by his friend James Boswell. These writings give a vivid picture of life in the 1700s.

king Frederick the Great. James did not return to England until George III took the throne.

James made many famous friends, among them great writers like Samuel Johnson and James Boswell, and artists like Joshua Reynolds. They shared his great love for people and they admired his work in agriculture and the business of growing crops.

Oglethorpe's colony in Georgia would see many changes long after he had returned to his native England, including the introduction of slavery. The settlers had become unhappy with the thought of growing their own crops while other colonies grew

Among Oglethorpe's many famous friends was Samuel Johnson, a leading scholar and author. Despite Johnson's poverty as a child and his lifelong illness, he excelled as a student and had a brilliant literary career.

Johnson was well-known for his sharp wit; he once said fishing was "a stick and a string, with a worm at one end and a fool on the other."

He published his *Dictionary of the English Language* in 1755. It was the first comprehensive English dictionary ever written. Noah Webster would publish the *American Dictionary of the English Language* 70 years later.

rich through the slaves who labored in the fields for them. With this change, Georgia grew in population and in size, eventually becoming a rich and powerful colony. Although these changes were not part of the ideal land that James Oglethorpe had in mind when he founded Georgia in 1733, he will forever remain the brave and clever leader who helped England's outcasts find a better life in the New World.

GLOSSARY

allies people who join in friendship

anxious worried or uneasy

christen to give a name; to baptize

contributions donations of money or help

court martial a court governed by military law

desperate extreme need

devoted strongly attached to something

establish to build or bring something into being

indentured a person who agrees to work for someone as repayment for a debt

persecution treating a person or group badly because of their ideas or religion

persuasion to be moved or urged by a person's idea

pirate robbers on the high seas

press-gang men commanded to force other men into military or naval service

rival a person you compete with

situation a place or circumstance

smuggle to bring goods illegally from another country

survive to continue to live

tradition cultural practices handed down from one generation to the next

treaties a formal agreement to have peace or end a war

CHRONOLOGY

1696 James Edward Oglethorpe is born on December 22.

1701 Enters Lompres Military Academy at age 15.

1703 Serves in Flanders.

1722 Elected as a member of the House of Commons.

1731 Attends Eton and Corpus Christi College, Oxford; receives honorary degree for philanthropy.

1732 Leads colonists to Georgia on the *Anne.*

1733 Establishes Savannah as the first European settlement in Georgia.

1734 The first Austrian settlers arrive to establish city of Ebenezer.

1735 Scottish Highlanders arrive to settle in city of Darien.

1739 The War of Jenkins' Ear flares up between England and Spain.

1740 Troops attack the Spanish at St. Augustine.

1742 Oglethorpe's Native American friends and the Scottish Highlanders win the Battle of the Bloody Marsh, marking the end of Spanish claims to England's southern colonies.

1743 Marries Lady Elizabeth Wright on September 15.

1747 Promoted to lieutenant-general.

1754 Retires from Parliament.

1785 Dies at the age of 89.

COLONIAL TIME LINE

1607 Jamestown, Virginia, is settled by the English.

1620 Pilgrims on the *Mayflower* land at Plymouth, Massachusetts.

1623 The Dutch settle New Netherlands, the colony that later becomes New York.

1630 Massachusetts Bay Colony is started.

1634 Maryland is settled as a Roman Catholic colony. Later Maryland becomes a safe place for people with different religious beliefs.

1636 Roger Williams is thrown out of the Massachusetts Bay Colony. He settles Rhode Island, the first colony to give people freedom of religion.

1682 William Penn forms the colony of Pennsylvania.

1688 Pennsylvania Quakers make the first formal protest against slavery.

1692 Trials for witchcraft are held in Salem, Massachusetts.

1712 Slaves revolt in New York. Twenty-one blacks are killed as punishment.

1720 Major smallpox outbreak occurs in Boston. Cotton Mather and some doctors try a new treatment. Many people think the new treatment shouldn't be used.

1754 French and Indian War begins. It ends nine years later.

1761 Benjamin Banneker builds a wooden clock that keeps precise time.

1765 Britain passes the Stamp Act. Violent protests break out in the colonies. The Stamp Act is ended the next year.

1775 The battles of Lexington and Concord begin the American Revolution.

1776 Declaration of Independence is signed.

FURTHER READING

Barrett, Tracy. *Growing up in Colonial America*. Brookfield, CT: Millbrook Press, 1995.

Brown, Ira L. *The Georgia Colony*. New York: Cromwell-Collier Press, 1970.

Fradin, Dennis Brindell. *The Georgia Colony*. New York: Children's Press, 1990.

Masters, Nancy Robinson. *Georgia*. New York: Children's Press, 1999.

Thompson, Kathleen. *Georgia*. Chatham, NJ: Raintree/Steck-Vaughn, 1996.

Vaeth, Gordon J. *The Man Who Founded Georgia*. New York: Cromwell-Collier Press, 1968.

Washburn, Carolyn K. *Multicultural Portrait of Colonial Life*. New York: Marshall Cavendish Corp., 1994.

INDEX

INDEX

PICTURE CREDITS

ABOUT THE AUTHOR

COOKIE LOMMEL started her career as a journalist in the entertainment industry. She has interviewed hundreds of film, television, and music personalities as an on-camera reporter for CNN. Cookie has written three other biographies for young adults, on Madame C. J. Walker, Robert Church, and Johnnie L. Cochran.

Senior Consulting Editor **ARTHUR M. SCHLESINGER, JR.** is the leading American historian of our time. He won the Pulitzer Prize for his book *The Age of Jackson* (1945) and again for *A Thousand Days* (1965). This chronicle of the Kennedy Administration also won a National Book Award. He has written many other books including a multi-volume series, *The Age of Roosevelt.* Professor Schlesinger is the Albert Schweitzer Professor of the Humanities at the City University of New York, and has been involved in several other Chelsea House projects, including the REVOLUTIONARY WAR LEADERS biographies on the most prominent figures of early American history.